# AFTER YOU

## JANINE AMOS

D1127650

Published in the United States by Windmill Books (Alphabet Soup)
Windmill Books
303 Park Avenue South
Suite #1280
New York, NY 10010-3657

**Library of Congress Cataloging-in-Publication Data**

Amos, Janine
        After you / Janine Amos.
                p.    cm. - (Best behavior)
        Contents: Going to the park—Painting a picture—At the store.
        Summary: Three brief stories demonstrate the importance of waiting your turn.
        ISBN 978-1-60754-020-5 (lib.) - 978-1-60754-032-8 (pbk.)
978-1-60754-033-5 (6 pack)
        1. Courtesy—Juvenile literature   [1. Etiquette  2. Conduct of life] I. Title  II. Series
        395.1'22—dc22

American Library Binding 13-digit ISBN: 978-1-60754-020-5
Paperback 13-digit ISBN: 978-1-60754-032-8
6 pack 13-Digit ISBN: 978-1-60754-033-5

Manufactured in China

**Credits:**
Editor: Louise John
Designer: Mark Holt
Photography: Gareth Boden
Production: Jenny Mulvanney

With thanks to:
Charlie Jenkins, Alex Williams, Sarah and Bejamin Collins, Charlie Simmons, Danyella Bessasa, Alex
Graham, Leon Williams, Kenneth Lycett, and Bobby.

Special thanks to the Coop store for allowing us to take photographs on their premises.

# Going to the Park

They are in a hurry to start their game.

5

The boys reach the park gate.

6

So do Mrs. Collins and Ben.
The gate is narrow.

Charlie pushes through.

How does Mrs. Collins feel?

Alex waits and lets them through.

After you.

Alex catches up with his friend.

12

# Painting a Picture

# Will and Jessica are painting.

They both go to wash their brushes.

# The paintings are spoiled.

# Will and Jessica start again.

18

Will thinks about it.

# At the Store

Sophie and Molly want to buy some candy.

The store is busy.

24

The big boys take his turn.

How does Mr. Jones feel?

*After you.*

The girls think about Mr. Jones.
They let him go first.

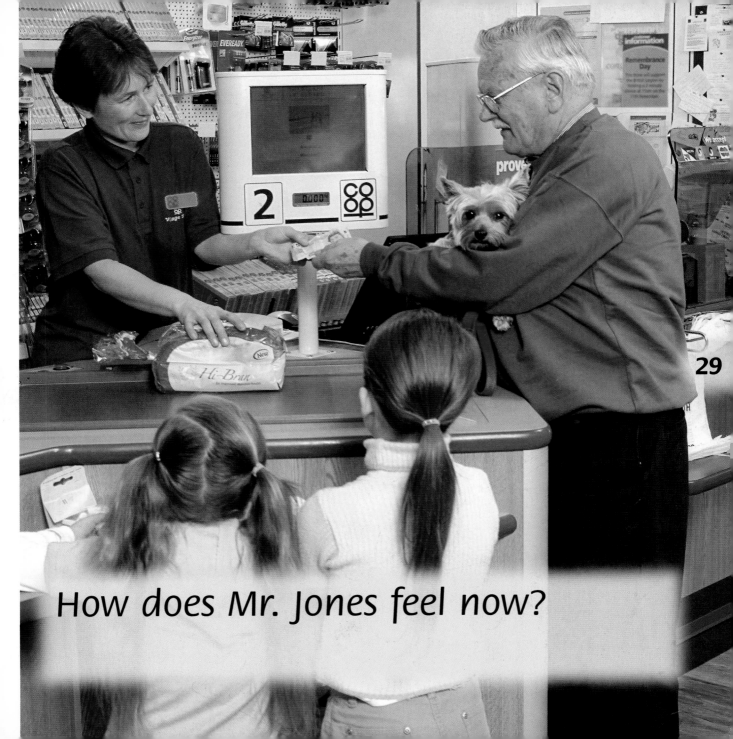

How does Mr. Jones feel now?

It makes things easier if someone waits.

Saying After you tells the other person you'll wait. It shows them you care.

## FOR FURTHER READING

INFORMATION BOOKS

Leaf, Munro. *Manners Can Be Fun*. New York: Universe, 2004.

Mattern, Joanne. *Do You Help Others*? New York: Weekly Reader Early Learning Library, 2007.

FICTION

Keller, Laurie. *Do Unto Otters: A Book About Manners*. New York: Henry Holt & Co., 2007.

**AUTHOR BIO**
Janine has worked in publishing as an editor and author, as a lecturer in education. Her interests are in personal growth and raising self-esteem and she works with educators, child psychologists and specialists in mediation. She has written more than fifty books for children. Many of her titles deal with first time experiences and emotional health issues such as Bullying, Death, and Divorce.

You can find more great fiction and nonfiction from Windmill Books at windmillbks.com